Cambridge English Qualifications

Pre A1 Starters

Practice Tests Plus

Second Edition

Teaching
not just testing

Marcella Banchetti
with Elaine Boyd

Pearson

Pearson Education Limited
KAO Two
KAO Park
Harlow
Essex
CM17 9NA
England
and Associated Companies throughout the world.

pearsonELT.com/practicetestsplus

© Pearson Education Limited 2018

First edition text by Marcella Banchetti. Second edition prepared by Elaine Boyd.

Typeset by Hart McLeod Ltd
Illustrated by John Batten, pages 5, 8, 9, 13, 16, 17, 23, 41, 59, 75, 77, 80, 93; all other illustrations by Quadrum Solutions.
Cover Image reproduced here by permission of Cambridge ESOL. This image is drawn from the CYLE Tests Sample Papers, published by Cambridge ESOL, 2006.

First published 2012
Second edition 2018

British Library Cataloguing in Publication Data
A catalogue record for this book is available from the British Library

ISBN 978 1 292 24028 2

Printed in Slovakia by Neografia

Note from the publisher
Pearson has robust editorial processes, including answer and fact checks, to ensure the accuracy of the content in this publication, and every effort is made to ensure this publication is free of errors. We are, however, only human, and occasionally errors do occur. Pearson is not liable for any misunderstandings that arise as a result of errors in this publication, but it is our priority to ensure that the content is accurate. If you spot an error, please do contact us at resourcescorrections@pearson.com so we can make sure it is corrected.

Contents

– Test 1 –

Listening.. 5
Reading & Writing... 11
Speaking.. 19

– Test 2 –

Listening.. 23
Reading & Writing... 29
Speaking.. 37

– Test 3 –

Listening.. 41
Reading & Writing... 47
Speaking.. 55

– Test 4 –

Listening.. 59
Reading & Writing... 65
Speaking.. 73

– Test 5 –

Listening.. 77
Reading & Writing... 83
Speaking.. 91

– Test 1 –

– Test 2 –

– Test 3 –

– Test 4 –

– Test 5 –

Part 1
– 5 questions –

Listen and draw lines. There is one example.

Alex   Eva   Hugo   Lucy

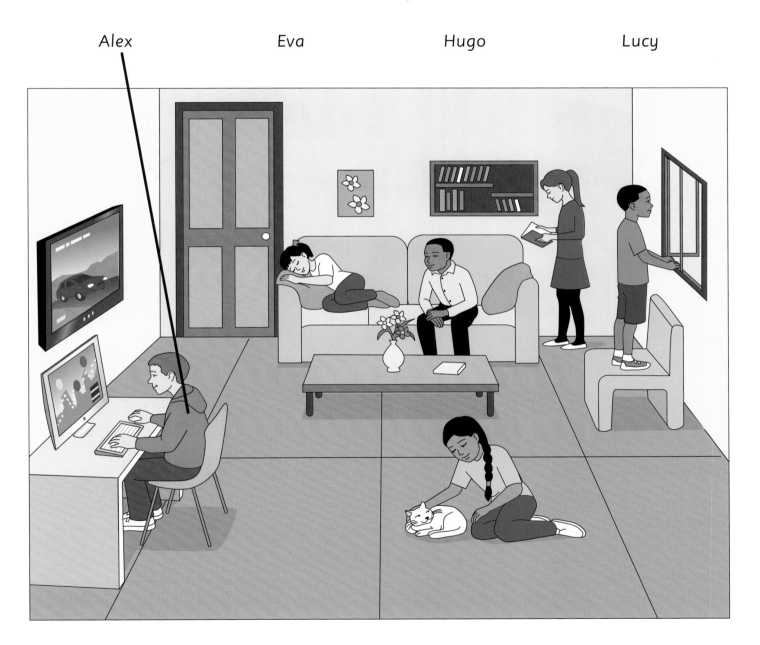

Tom   Sue   Sam

Part 2
– 5 questions –

Read the question. Listen and write a name or a number.
There are two examples.

Examples

What is the girl's name?   _Lucy_

How old is she?   _6_

Questions

1   How many dolls has Lucy got?   _____

2   What's the dog's name?   _____

3   Which class is Lucy in?   _____

4   What's the name of Lucy's school?   _____ School

5   How many children are in Lucy's class?   _____

Part 3
– 5 questions –

Listen and tick (✓) the box. There is one example.

What's Nick doing?

A ☐

B ✓

C ☐

1   Which boy is Tom?

A ☐

B ☐

C ☐

2   Which is Jill's favourite drink?

A ☐

B ☐

C ☐

3   What's Mark doing?

A

B

C

4   Where's the spider?

A

B

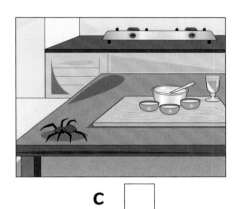

C

5   Where's the baby's duck?

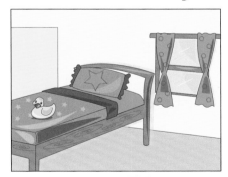

A

B

C

Part 4
– 5 questions –

Listen and colour. There is one example.

Part 1
– 5 questions –

Look and read. Put a tick (✓) or a cross (X) in the box.
There are two examples.

Examples

This is a burger.

This is an orange.

Questions

1

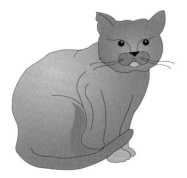

This is a cow. []

2

This is a doll.

☐

3

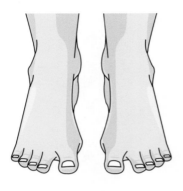

These are socks.

☐

4

This is a fish.

☐

5

These are watermelons.

☐

Part 2
– 5 questions –

Look and read. Write yes or no.

Examples

There are four children in the room.   *yes*

There is a dog under the table.   *no*

Questions

1   There is a mouse in the room.   _____

2   A boy is playing with a train.   _____

3   There are blue flowers on the bookcase.   _____

4   A baby is holding a ball.   _____

5   The children are watching television.   _____

Part 3
– 5 questions –

Look at the pictures. Look at the letters. Write the words.

Example

<u>b o o k</u>

Questions

1

_ _ _ _

2

_ _ _ _ _

3

_ _ _ _ _

4

_ _ _ _ _ _

5

_ _ _ _ _ _

Part 4
– 5 questions –

Read this. Choose a word from the box. Write the correct word next to the numbers 1–5. There is one example.

Monkeys

Monkeys live in the _____*trees*_____ with their family and friends.

Monkeys are fun. They can run and jump with their long **(1)** _____ .

They eat fruit but **(2)** _____ are their favourite food. Lots of

monkeys are small but they have long **(3)** _____ . They are brown

or orange and have big **(4)** _____ . They have ten fingers and ten

(5) _____ , like people. Monkeys are very funny!

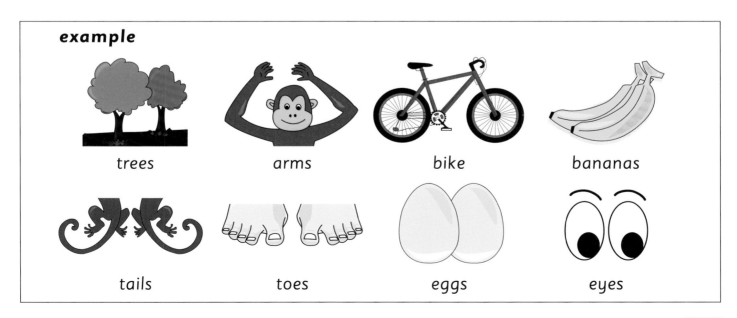

example

| trees | arms | bike | bananas |

| tails | toes | eggs | eyes |

Part 5
– 5 questions –

Look at the pictures and read the questions. Write one-word answers.

Examples

Where are the people? in the _____street_____

How many shops are there? _____three_____

Questions

1 What is the woman holding? a _____

2   Where are the jeans?   on the _____

3   What is the girl in the blue
     dress looking at?   at a _____

4   Where are the people now?   in front of a _____

5   What are they holding?   some big _____

Object cards

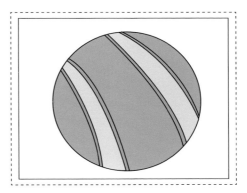

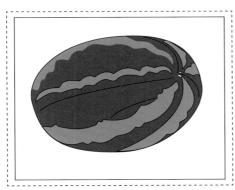

STARTERS SPEAKING. Scene Picture

Part 1
– 5 questions –

Listen and draw lines. There is one example.

Alice   Ben   Kim   Mark

Grace   Nick   Anna

Part 2
– 5 questions –

Read the question. Listen and write a name or a number.

There are two examples.

Examples

What's the girl's name? _____ *Anna* _____

How old is she? _____ *8* _____

Questions

1   What is Anna's mum's name?   _____

2   How old is Anna's brother?   _____

3   What's his name?   _____

4   What's the name of Anna's sister?   _____

5   How old is Anna's sister?   _____

Part 3
– 5 questions –

Listen and tick (✓) the box. There is one example.

Which girl is Anna?

A ☐

B ☐

C ✓

1   What's Bill's favourite toy?

A ☐

B ☐

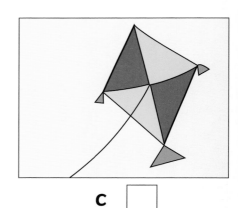

C ☐

2   What's Pat's grandfather doing?

A ☐

B ☐

C ☐

3   What can May do?

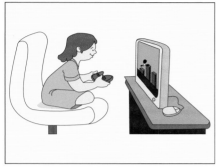

A ☐

B ☐

C ☐

4   What does Grace want?

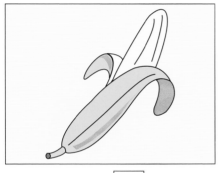

A ☐

B ☐

C ☐

5   Where's the television?

A ☐

B ☐

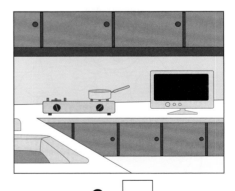

C ☐

Part 4
– 5 questions –

Listen and colour. There is one example.

Part 1
– 5 questions –

**Look and read. Put a tick (✓) or a cross (✗) in the box.
There are two examples.**

Examples

This is a guitar.

This is a table.

Questions

1

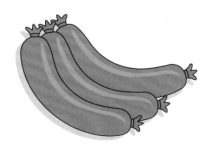

These are sausages. ☐

2

This is a shirt.

☐

3

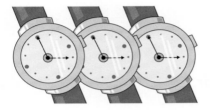

These are radios.

☐

4

These are windows.

☐

5

This is a kitchen.

☐

Part 2
– 5 questions –

Look and read. Write yes or no.

Examples

The woman is wearing a skirt.   _yes_

The boy on the beach is running.   _no_

Questions

1   The boat is green and red.   _____

2   A boy is swimming in the water.   _____

3   The monkey is fishing.   _____

4   A man is sleeping under a tree.   _____

5   The woman is reading a book.   _____

Part 3
– 5 questions –

Look at the pictures. Look at the letters. Write the words.

Example

<u>d o g</u>

o	g	d

Questions

1

_ _ _

w	o	c

2

_ _ _ _ _

k	s	a	n	e

3

_ _ _ _ _

p	e	h	e	s

4

_ _ _ _ _ _

z	d	a	r	i	l

5

_ _ _ _ _ _ _

n	c	h	e	k	c	i

Part 4
– 5 questions –

Read this. Choose a word from the box. Write the correct word next to the numbers 1–5. There is one example.

Cats

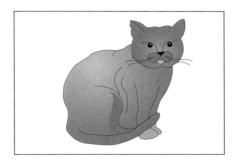

Cats live in _____*houses*_____ but they like playing in the **(1)** _____

with **(2)** _____ .

They can be many colours – black, white, brown, grey. They are not very big, they have four legs and a tail and they can run.

Lots of cats sleep on a **(3)** _____ in the hall. They drink **(4)** _____

and water and they love **(5)** _____ . Cats don't like dogs!

example

houses   milk   apples   legs

fish   garden   children   mat

Part 5
– 5 questions –

Look at the pictures and read the questions. Write one-word answers.

Examples

How many people are there
in the picture?   _____ four _____

Where is the food?   next to the _____ car _____

Questions

1   What are the children doing?   _____

2   Where are the children now?   in the _____

3   Who has got the ball?   the _____

4   Where are the father and the dog sleeping?   under a _____

5   What is the boy doing now?   _____ a sausage

Object cards

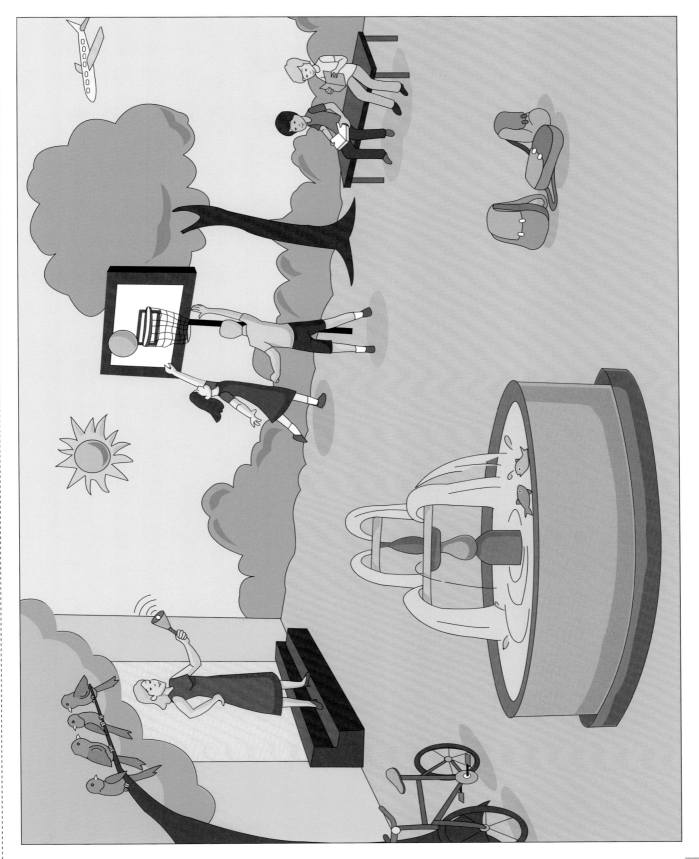

STARTERS SPEAKING. Scene Picture

Part 1
– 5 questions –

Listen and draw lines. There is one example.

Bill   Jill   Dan   Pat

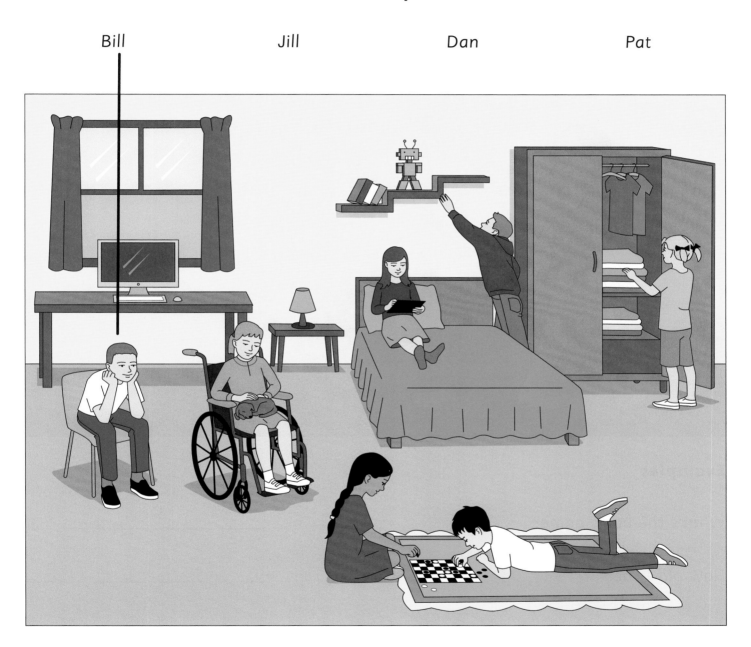

Matt   May   Tom

Part 2
– 5 questions –

Read the question. Listen and write a name or a number.

There are two examples.

Examples

What's the boy's name?   Bill

How old is he?   7

Questions

1   What is Bill's friend's name?   _____

2   Which class are the children in at school?   _____

3   How many cats are in Bill's house?   _____

4   What's the name of Bill's favourite cat?   _____

5   How many chickens has Bill's friend got?   _____

Part 3
– 5 questions –

Listen and tick (✓) the box. There is one example.

What's Lucy doing?

A ☐

B ☐

C ✓

1   What does Ben want?

A ☐

B ☐

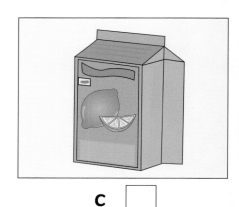

C ☐

2   Which is Nick?

A ☐

B ☐

C ☐

3   What's for breakfast?

A ☐

B ☐

C ☐

4   Where is Anna's pen?

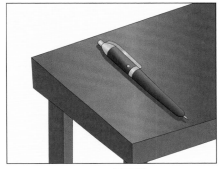

A ☐

B ☐

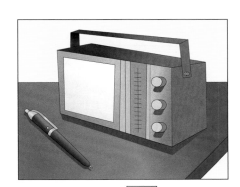

C ☐

5   Which book would Sam like?

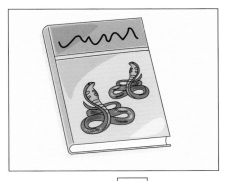

A ☐

B ☐

C ☐

Part 4
– 5 questions –

Listen and colour. There is one example.

Part 1
– 5 questions –

Look and read. Put a tick (✓) or a cross (✗) in the box.
There are two examples.

Examples

This is a flower.   ✓

This is a television.   ✗

Questions

1

This is an eraser.

2

These are goats.

☐

3

This is a potato.

☐

4

This is a motorbike.

☐

5

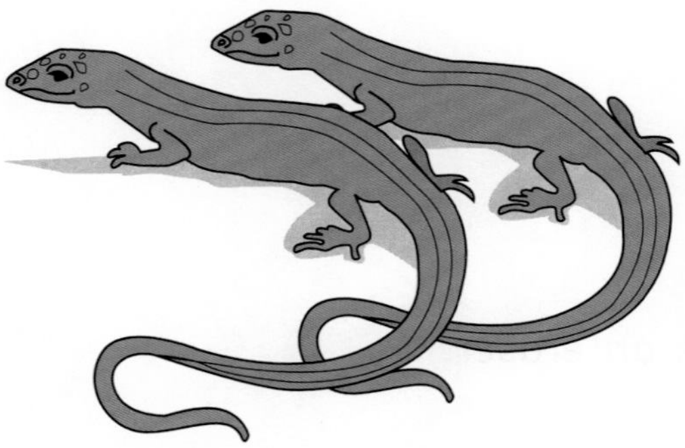

These are snakes.

☐

Part 2
– 5 questions –

Look and read. Write yes or no.

Examples

There are two orange trees.   *yes*

The birds are flying.   *no*

Questions

1   The boy has got four oranges.   _____

2   The apples on the tree are green.   _____

3   There are watermelons in a blue bag.   _____

4   A lizard is sleeping under the pear tree. _____

5   A girl is picking up a tomato.   _____

Part 3
– 5 questions –

Look at the pictures. Look at the letters. Write the words.

Example

<u>c h i p s</u>

Questions

1

_ _ _ _

2

_ _ _ _

3

_ _ _ _ _

4

_ _ _ _ _ _

5

_ _ _ _ _ _ _ _ _

Part 4
– 5 questions –

Read this. Choose a word from the box. Write the correct word next to the numbers 1–5. There is one example.

Parks

Parks are big with a lot of _____trees_____ and **(1)** _____ .

Lots of parks have a playground. **(2)** _____ can run and play in parks.

They can ride **(3)** _____ and fly kites in parks.

In the trees there are a lot of **(4)** _____ – black, blue and green.

Many parks have water and ducks and children can give food to them.

Parks open in the **(5)** _____ and close in the evening.

Part 5
– 5 questions –

Look at the pictures and read the questions. Write one-word answers.

Examples

What is the teacher wearing?   a ___skirt___

How many children are there?   ___five___

Questions

1   What is the boy with the red T-shirt doing?   _____ a ball

2   Who is holding the ball?   the _____

3   What are the children looking at?   a _____

4   Where are the children now?   in the _____

5   What is the teacher doing?   _____ to the board

Object cards

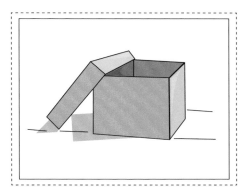

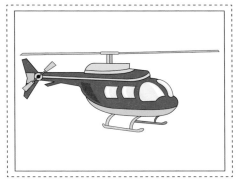

Part 1
– 5 questions –

Listen and draw lines. There is one example.

Anna   Nick   Dan   Eva

Sam   Kim   Tom

Part 2
– 5 questions –

Read the question. Listen and write a name or a number.

There are two examples.

Examples

What's the boy's name?   Sam

How old is he?   10

Questions

1   What is Sam's mum's name?   _____

2   What's the name of Sam's grandfather?   _____

3   How old is Sam's sister?   _____

4   How many brothers has Sam got?   _____

5   Where does Sam go to school?   _____ Wall School

Part 3
– 5 questions –

Listen and tick (✓) the box. There is one example.

Which is Tom's brother?

A   **B** ☐   **C** ☐

1   What does Pat like doing?

A ☐   **B** ☐   **C** ☐

2   Which is Matt's house?

A ☐   **B** ☐   **C**

3   What's Lucy's dad doing?

A ☐

B ☐

C ☐

4   What animals has Sue's grandmother got?

A ☐

B ☐

C ☐

5   Where is Kim's dad?

A ☐

B ☐

C ☐

Part 4
– 5 questions –

Listen and colour. There is one example.

Part 1
– 5 questions –

Look and read. Put a tick (✓) or a cross (✗) in the box.
There are two examples.

Examples

This is a ball.

This is a horse.

Questions

1

This is a bus.

2

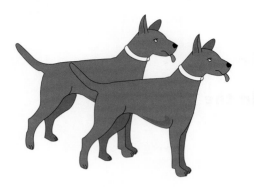

These are cats.

☐

3

These are frogs.

☐

4

This is a table.

☐

5

These are guitars.

☐

Part 2
– 5 questions –

Look and read. Write yes or no.

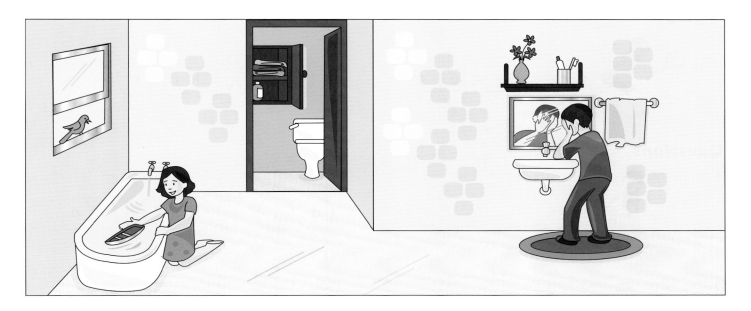

Examples

There is a mirror on the wall.   _yes_

The window is open.   _no_

Questions

1   The girl is playing with a boat.   _____

2   There is a blue bird flying.   _____

3   The door of the cupboard is closed.   _____

4   The mat is red and blue.   _____

5   The boy is washing his hair.   _____

Part 3
– 5 questions –

Look at the pictures. Look at the letters. Write the words.

Example

<u>t e n n i s</u>

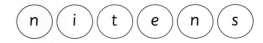

Questions

1

_ _ _ _ _ _ _

2

_ _ _ _ _ _ _

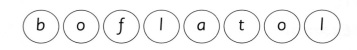

3

_ _ _ _ _ _ _

4

_ _ _ _ _ _ _

5

_ _ _ _ _ _ _ _

Part 4
– 5 questions –

Read this. Choose a word from the box. Write the correct word next to the numbers 1–5. There is one example.

Televisions

People have televisions in their _____*houses*_____ . They can be in the

bedroom, kitchen or the **(1)** _____ . A television can be on a

(2) _____ or a cupboard or on a wall. Televisions can be big or

small. A lot of people watch television in the **(3)** _____ . People sit

on a **(4)** _____ or on the floor in front of the television.

(5) _____ like watching television and can learn about the world.

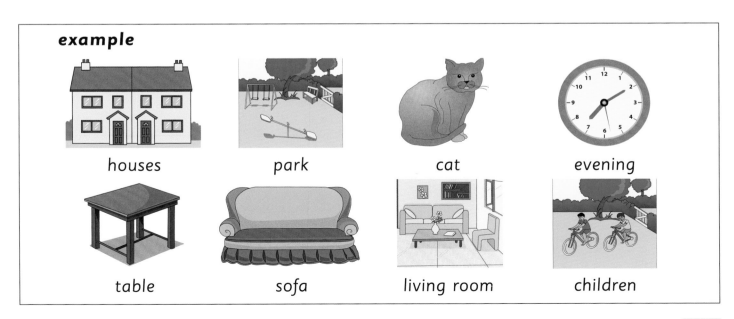

example			
houses	park	cat	evening
table	sofa	living room	children

Part 5
– 5 questions –

Look at the pictures and read the questions. Write one-word answers.

Examples

Where are the fish?   in the _____ water _____

How many fish are there?   _____ six _____

Questions

1   What is the boy holding?   a _____

2   What is the dog doing?   it's _____

3   What has the girl got?   a _____

4   Where is the dog?   under a _____

5   How many birds are there on the trees?   _____

Object cards

STARTERS SPEAKING. Scene Picture

Part 1
– 5 questions –

Listen and draw lines. There is one example.

Matt   Pat   Hugo   Sue

Alex   Alice   Mark

Part 2
– 5 questions –

Read the question. Listen and write a name or a number.

There are two examples.

Examples

What is the dog's name?   _Tom_

How old is it?   _4_

Questions

1   What is the girl's name?   _____

2   What's the name of her school?   _____ House School

3   Who does she sit next to?   _____

4   How many goats has she got?   _____

5   How many hippos are in the book?   _____

Part 3
– 5 questions –

Listen and tick (✓) the box. There is one example.

What's Hugo doing?

A ☐

B ☐

C ✓

1   Where's Jill?

A ☐

B ☐

C ☐

2   What is dad's favourite game?

A ☐

B ☐

C ☐

3   Where's grandpa?

A

B

C

4   What can Anna have for lunch today?

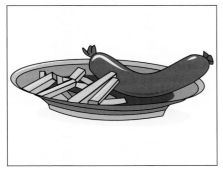

A

B

C

5   What's Sam doing?

A

B

C

Part 4
– 5 questions –

Listen and colour. There is one example.

Part 1
– 5 questions –

Look and read. Put a tick (✓) or a cross (✗) in the box.
There are two examples.

Examples

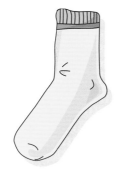

This is a sock.

This is a leg.

Questions

1

This is a shell.

2

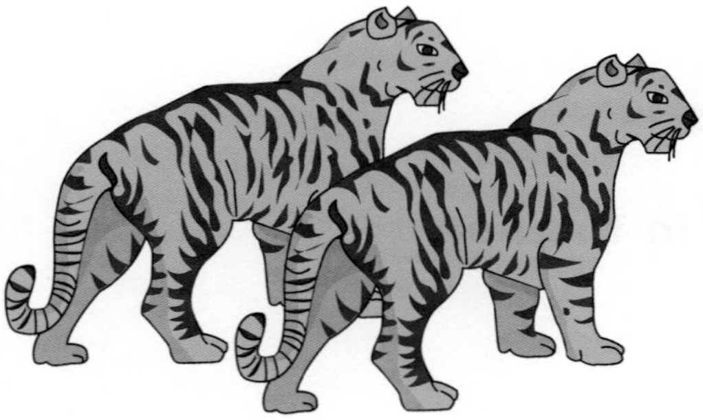

These are crocodiles.

3

These are hats.

4

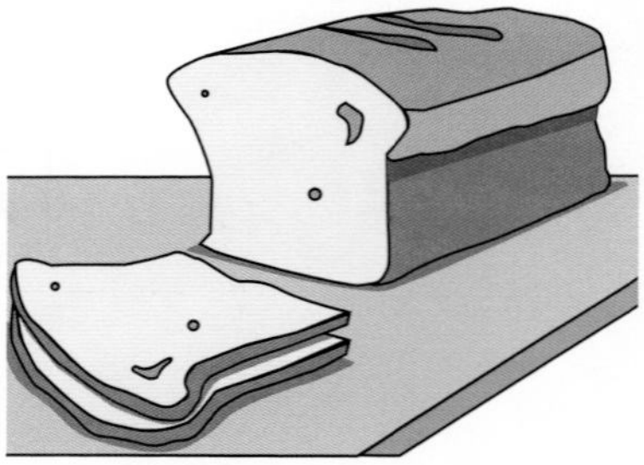

This is a cake.

5

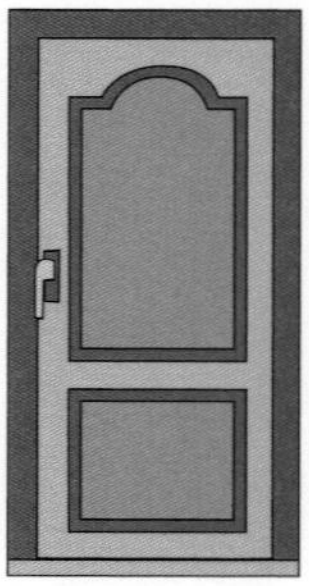

This is a door.

Part 2
– 5 questions –

Look and read. Write yes or no.

Examples

There are two boys in the room.

yes

There is a green kite under the bed.

no

Questions

1   One of the boys is reading a book.

2   There is a clock on the wall.

3   There are three apples on the table.

4   The doll is between the ball and the cat.

5   There is a television on the cupboard.

Part 3
– 5 questions –

Look at the pictures. Look at the letters. Write the words.

Example

<u>d o o r</u>

| o | r | o | d |

Questions

1

_ _ _ _

| e | k | s | d |

2

_ _ _ _ _ _

| i | n | w | o | d | w |

3

_ _ _ _ _ _ _

| d | o | b | r | m | e | o |

4

_ _ _ _ _ _ _ _

| m | a | r | c | i | r | h | a |

5

_ _ _ _ _ _ _ _

| t | h | o | m | b | o | a | r |

Part 4
– 5 questions –

Read this. Choose a word from the box. Write the correct word next to the numbers 1–5. There is one example.

Tables

Tables are in the _____ *kitchen* _____ , the living room and in the

(1) _____ too. Tables can be big or small and people sit on

(2) _____ next to the table. Tables can be a lot of different colours

and they have got three or four legs.

People can put food on tables and children can read **(3)** _____ at

tables. A lot of people work on their **(4)** _____ on tables.

(5) _____ sleep under tables.

example

kitchen	trees	cats	books
garden	carrot	chairs	computers

Part 5
– 5 questions –

Look at the pictures and read the questions. Write one-word answers.

Examples

How many children are there? _____ five

Where are the people? at the _____ zoo

Questions

1   Where is the monkey? on a _____

2   What are the girls looking at?   the _____

3   Who's got the teacher's bag?   the _____

4   Where is the teacher now?   under the _____

5   What is the crocodile eating?   a _____

Object cards

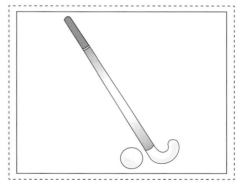

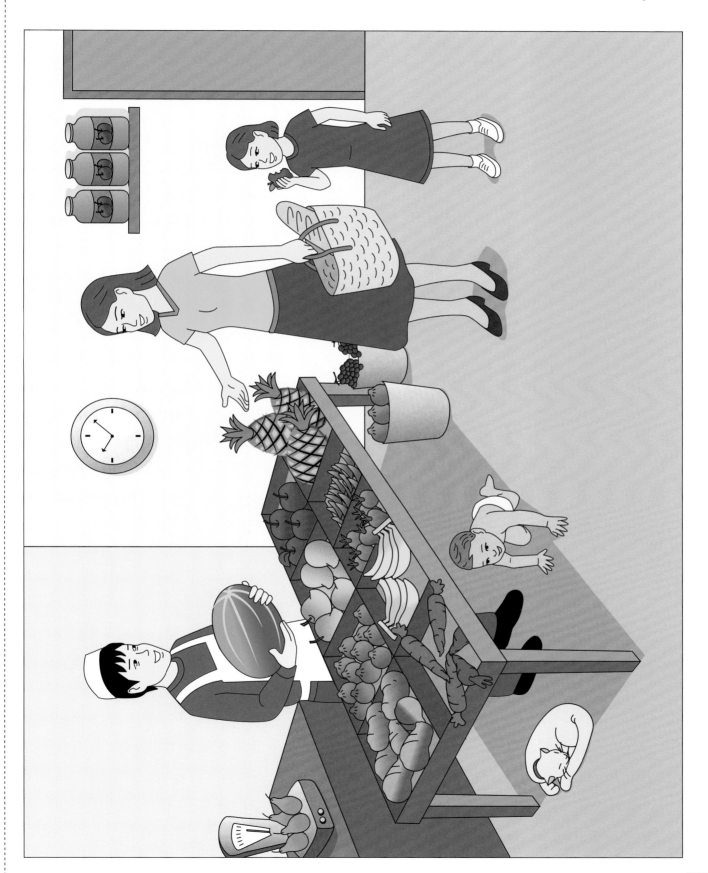

STARTERS SPEAKING. Scene Picture